MW01135720

How to Be Your Own Travel Agent

How to Be Your Own Travel Agent

A practical guide to vacation-planning for the
independent traveler

Nina Thomas

2017

Copyright © 2017 by Nina Thomas

Traveling with Nina

travelingwithnina.com

All rights reserved. This book or any portion thereof may not be reproduced, stored in a retrieval system, transmitted, or used in any manner whatsoever without the express written permission of the author except for the use of brief quotations in the book for review or presentation material. All pictures used in this book are owned by the author.

First Printing: 2017

ISBN – 13: 978-1975713768

ISBN-10: 1975713761

Nina Thomas

Dedications

I would like to dedicate this book to my husband, Jared, who is my steady travel partner. I didn't come up with these tips and tricks all on my own. We have learned so many things together. He is (and always will be) my favorite person to travel with.

I would also like to dedicate this book to everyone who has said they can't afford to travel or don't know how to plan a trip. This book is for you.

Contents

Introduction

On our first trip overseas, my husband and I hired a travel agency to book everything for us. We had no idea what we were doing, and trusted their judgment. We paid a hefty fee for their expertise, and ended up with some overpriced hotels in not-so-convenient locations, flights with long layovers and some misunderstandings that cost us a lot of money (such as paying the driver twice for a ride from the airport).

The travel agency offered few customizable options, but when I really thought about what they provided, it wasn't much. In fact, I was given fewer options than if I had organized the trip myself. The company booked flights, hotels and ground transportation. Everything else, we did on our own (aka struggled through it.)

Booking flights, hotels and ground transportation is not complicated. If you don't know what you're doing, hiring a tour company seems like a better option. But, I'm here to tell you that you can do this on your own. Perhaps all you need are some suggestions regarding how to plan trips on your own.

Traveling with Nina was born after realizing there were so many practical things I wished I had known a long time ago. I don't pretend to be some travel guru or expert, but there many things I've learned by mistake and over time that I think are helpful to others. I hope that you can learn from my mistakes, and be better prepared for your next vacation. Traveling has been one of my favorite hobbies, and perhaps it's one of yours too. However, it may seem like a daunting task to plan a trip for yourself, because after all, you're no expert. But here's a little secret: I'm no expert either. I've learned how to plan trips, just like I want to help you learn how to plan your own trips.

I began writing articles for a blog that have proven to be helpful to travelers, and this book is a result of working with travelers through my blog postings. My desire is to empower others to plan trips for themselves, without needing to rely on travel agents to do it for them. Instead of letting someone else decide the type of traveler you will be, you get to decide. You know who you are, what you want, how you function best on a trip, what types of hotels you like, what you want out of this vacation, and so on and so on. You know if you're a camper or a luxury hotel dweller. You know if you would never wake up at 4 a.m. to catch a 6 a.m. flight, even if it meant saving $500. You know if you hate road trips. Whatever it is, you know what kind of traveling you want to do, so you're the best person to plan a trip for you. The best thing I can do is give you practical advice on how to plan the trip that makes sense for you. I love being able to give tips and advice to others so they can feel like they're capable of doing it themselves. Basically, it's this old Chinese proverb: "Give a man a fish and you feed him for a day. Teach a man to fish and you feed him for a lifetime." It may seem daunting, or frustrating, or complicated, but it really isn't. One of my proudest moments was when a friend sent me their planned itinerary for a trip. They were so excited, they used my tips, and were able to do it all on their own. I had empowered her to plan her own dream trip. Turns out, she had it in her all along! Just a few nudges in the right direction, and bam, her dream trip all thought out the way she wanted it to go. You don't need a travel agent; you are capable of doing this on your own! You can be your very own travel agent. You can take yourself on the vacation of your dreams.

The tips in this book will work for you no matter what kind of traveler you are. There are a lot of books on "budget traveling" or "luxury traveling". I have to tell you that sometimes I'm both. Sometimes I plan a cheap bare-bones trip; sometimes I plan an extravagant trip. Maybe you're not a one-size-fits-all type of traveler. Since you're designing your own trip, you can pick and choose whatever you want! You don't have to decide you're this type of traveler or that type of traveler. You can just design a trip around your interests, how much you want to spend and what you like. You get to tailor-make your own trip. I'm going to tell you how to find the stuff you're looking for, so you can have the trip that is personalized for you.

Take note: In this book, I mention online sources that I find useful and helpful. These are all my personal opinions. I am under no obligation, nor am I being paid to promote them. I am giving you my honest opinions of what sources I use, and why I use them. I'm sure there are many other wonderful websites, but these have been ones I find useful and helpful, and that is why I mention them here.

How exactly do you plan a trip?

I get frustrated when I see a lot of inspirational travel quotes, and cool pictures of people on a remote island somewhere and I have no idea a. how they got there, b. how I can get there, or c. how much it costs. I'm a practical person. I want details. There are a lot of travelers who want to inspire others to travel. I'm more interested in getting you the details on how you can actually plan a trip once you've been "inspired" to do so. Without the how-to-do-it, it's sort of like telling someone who knows very little about soccer to "get out there and make a goal!"

I'm not going to just tell you to "plan a trip" I'm going to do my best to tell you *how to* plan a trip. As I said in the introduction, I want to empower you to plan a trip. You know what you want to see (and if you don't, I'll even help with that), you need help to sit down and actually plan the darn thing. In this book, you become your own travel agent by learning how to:

- Select an appropriate travel destination for you
- Design an itinerary
- Create a travel budget
- Do research for your trip
- Book flights and accommodations

There are a lot of other things I could talk about in terms of traveling, but to me, this is the most practical side of traveling. If you can figure out these things, you can design your own trip to your exact specifications. You can get destination-specific guides that give you details on the places you're going, read endless blogs and books on all sorts of travel-related things, look at beautiful pictures all day... but right now, you just need some simple, practical advice on how to plan a trip. I hope this guide helps you to K.I.S.S. (keep it simple, stupid.)

Selecting a destination

I select where I want to go through research. I find inspiration from other travelers on Instagram, Twitter and blogs. I read travel books from the library. I look at TripAdvisor for popular destinations or "destinations on the rise." I Google things I'm interested in to see where in the world I could view those things; such as beaches with a lot of shells, art museums that feature a lot of impressionist paintings, treks with some of the best views in the world. You may be surprised at some of the places that actually exist. As you discover these places, write them down, bookmark them, pin them, screenshot them... keep a record of them however it makes sense to you.

Perhaps you've been inspired by a beautiful photograph from Italy, your friends' travel stories from Canada or a magazine article you read about NYC. Hopefully you have compiled that list of wonderful, beautiful and exciting places to go! Now what? If it's a long list, this may be daunting. It's especially daunting if you're an indecisive person. If I can go anywhere, and I want to go everywhere, how do I decide? Depending on a number of factors, you can narrow down the list of where to go on your next trip. If you already have a place in mind, you can skip these questions. However, if you are trying to decide where to go, use these series of questions as a way to narrow it down:

Where do you want to go?

Have your list handy of places that you really want to go. For right now, pay no attention to cost, time of year, flight time or any other deterrents. Did I really just say *pay no attention to cost?* You'll see as you continue reading this book that money is something we can work through. Once you plan your itinerary and travel budget, you know what to save for. If you realize you'll have to save for two years for that trip, there are ways to trim down the travel budget and ways you can trim down your own weekly budget to save for this trip. Money is rarely my deterrent; because I know how many options are out there. So at this stage, I say dream big!

What was your favorite thing about your last trip?

Take a moment to think back on your last trip and what it was that you loved about it. For example, was it seeing a particular museum? Was it the day when you had nothing planned and you stumbled onto a beautiful beach? Was it the food you ate? Was it a long hike? What was it? Don't just think about the activity itself, but the essence of the activity. For example, let's say you liked hiking the most. What is it about the hike that you liked? Just being outside? Conquering a fear? Seeing the heights? Being somewhere new? Look for *why* this activity was your favorite. This will help you see if the destination you select can help you achieve your most favorite part about traveling.

What was your least favorite thing about your last trip?

This is probably easier to answer than your favorite thing, because we're usually good at complaining. However, there's probably at least one thing that stands out the most. Maybe there were many things, but what was the worst part? Too many activities jammed into one day? Too much travel time? The hotels were terrible? You hated the food? You never felt relaxed? You were bored out of your mind? What was it? And again, look for *why* that was so upsetting to you. I often hear people reflect on a trip and say they will "never go back to such and such place again." When you pick it apart, it's typically not the destination they had a problem with (sometimes it is) but something specific that they didn't like about it. If you're not a beach person, and you spent a week in the Dominican Republic, maybe it's not that you hate the country, but you hate going to the beach. Find out what it is that you don't like, and that will help you to narrow down the choices. (If you are having trouble with this portion, skip ahead to "ten reasons you hated your last vacation" to see if any of those describe your last vacation.)

Now that you've had time to think through your favorite and least favorite thing about your trip, you can look at your list of five choices and narrow it down. Are there places that would be mainly museums and you really didn't like that the last time? Are there places that are way too far to fly, and that was your least favorite part? Was there a place that has killer food and that's what you loved the last time? Narrow down as much as you can with these.

Can you go to multiple places on your list?

Maybe you had two places in Europe on the list and you could do them both in one trip. That would be a nice way to incorporate more than one place. However, if you have one destination in Europe, North America and Asia, you might be hard-pressed to squeeze all that in a week.

What time of year are you going on this trip?

Look at your list of places and consider the time of year. Are there things that you can't do in the place you want to go because you're not going at the right time? For example, if you really want to go to the Bahamas, you may not want to go during their hurricane season. Not all climates can be avoided, but if you know you want to lie on the beach all day, you might be in for a rude awakening going at a bad time of year.

With all these factors in consideration, you should have a pretty good idea of where you want to go. Now that you have a destination, it's time to start budgeting.

Practice Scenario
Russ and Kate pick a place to go

Russ and Kate live in Wisconsin. Russ has been working the same 9-5 job for six years, and Kate just finished earning her bachelor's degree. Money has been tight, but they've been working hard at trying to save. They've decided it's time to go on a vacation. They both have slightly different interests, but they enjoy being together. Russ likes to be outside, and when he's not outside, he's sort of a homebody. Kate loves paleontology, museums and fancy dinners. They both sat down and made a list of places they'd like to go. Prior to making their lists, they both did a little Google searching. Kate searched "places to see dinosaur bones" and saw a park in Canada and one in Colorado. Russ searched "best destinations for outdoor enthusiasts", and noticed a lot of national parks were on that list, as well as New Zealand. They both added those destinations to their lists. Here are their lists:

Russ	Kate
U.S. National Parks (in the west)	Egypt
New Zealand	Colorado
Canadian Rockies	Paris, France
Iceland	Dinosaur Provincial Park

Russ and Kate decided to go through the exercise to narrow down their destination choice. Russ' least favorite part of the last vacation he went on was the amount of travel time it took to get there, how tired he was after he got there and how short the trip was. Basically, the trip was too short for the amount of travel time. Kate's least favorite part of their last vacation was the bad food they ate, and not having enough to do during the day. Just sitting around a condo doesn't interest her. His favorite part

17

of the trip was whenever he was outside. He couldn't soak up enough beautiful views. Kate's favorite part was getting to read books about her interests. Since she wasn't doing a lot, she could at least learn while sitting. After discussing this, Russ realized that he wants to go somewhere that has amazing outdoor scenery. Kate wants to go somewhere where her mind is stimulated, and she's learning something hands-on. Since they know they don't want to have a lot of travel time (since Russ hated that) they've narrowed down the list to the Canadian Rockies, Colorado, U.S. National Parks and Dinosaur Provincial Park. They realized they could go to the Canadian Rockies and Dinosaur Park in one trip; it's only a 7 hr. drive between the two. However, they wanted to go somewhere in January, and it will be too cold there to spend a lot of time outside, so they decided to wait on that trip. That means, they are going to plan a trip to see some U.S. National Parks and Colorado. Russ wants to visit some parks with amazing scenery, and Kate wants to go to parks with learning centers and tour guides where she can learn the history and facts about the geological attributes. Both of them are excited about this trip. Now, they now just have to plan it.

Ten reasons you hated your last vacation

Your last vacation wasn't what you hoped it would be. You made endless travel mistakes, and you ran into things that were not in your control. If the following things have not happened to you on a trip, yet, just wait! These things don't have to make you hate your vacation, but sometimes they do. Some of these things can be avoided, and some of them can't. However, you decide how you're going to deal with these situations, which can make or break a vacation.

1. Driving time took a lot longer than Google maps said.

So Google maps said an hour right? I wish I had a dollar for every time this has happened to me. Driving in Ecuador, we quickly realized that if the GPS said 1 hour, it was actually going to be 2 hours. Or when we were driving in Yosemite, the traffic was so bad that a 20-minute trip was actually going to be an hour. You also have to account for driving behind farmer's trucks, and 15 mph dirt roads. So my recommendation is to not trust Google maps. They are helpful, but you'll be sorely disappointed if it says 5 minutes to get through Miami when really it's an hour. Google maps driving time is not to be trusted with your life.

2. Everyone was hungry and the food was terrible.

Add this one to the fact that Google maps said "20 minutes" and now it's an hour and everyone in the car is starving. Plus, you didn't research the restaurant's parking situation, so you have to wander around, trying to find parking. You pick the first place you find and it's terrible. Don't let this happen to you. PACK SNACKS. Plan your food accordingly. Do not invite "hanger" on vacation with you.

3. The weather didn't cooperate.

Weather is always unpredictable, but a little research on it ahead of time is helpful. If you're going somewhere in the USA in spring, it will most likely be rainy. So if you're upset that it's March and it's raining 5 out of the 6 days, well, there's not much that can be helped. Maybe you went in June and were shocked with a storm that couldn't be avoided. However, be prepared if you're going somewhere during a time when bad weather is to be expected. Have a rainy day plan. If you have all outdoor things scheduled, you'll be real disappointed. At least have a few places you can go if the weather isn't ideal.

4. You went with people that didn't have the same vacation philosophy as you do.

This one is hard to find out unless you ask a lot of questions ahead of time. If you're planning a trip and you are interested in sleeping and staying in the whole time, and the people you're planning with keep talking about "waking up at 6 a.m. to make it across town to the museum," you're going to have a frustrating vacation. Make sure you're all on the same page. If you can't in good conscience do what everyone wants to do, that's OK. Everyone has a different vacation style. Try to plan vacations with people who are flexible or into what you're into. It makes it a lot easier on everyone.

5. Your sleeping accommodations kept you up all night. Cheap accommodations usually mean cheap beds with thin walls. This ensures that you can toss and turn all night, and also hear the kegger going on in the room next door. If you're a light sleeper, you may need to shell out some extra money to make sure you get a good night's rest. If you have back problems or any other issues that could make sleeping anywhere but home difficult for you, you might want to pay for a nicer place. What kind of vacation is it, really, if you get 3 hours of sleep every night and are Mr./Mrs. Cranky Pants the whole trip?

6. You didn't think all that traveling would make you tired and cranky.

So you thought 20 hours in the airport would be fine because after all, you're not doing anything but resting. The fact is, though, it's not rest. Not real rest. Waking up to let someone next to you go to the bathroom, getting shook around by turbulence, and being woken up for pretzels every hour isn't exactly "relaxing." Traveling takes it out of you. You'll need rest from all your restless time on the plane.

7. Your airline lost your bags.

You thought all that "packing light" and only bringing a carry-on nonsense was for everyone else. Until, you went to baggage claim and waited for 30 minutes... that turned into 60 minutes... and your bag never came. Then you get to fill out paperwork for another hour, after you've waited in a long line with the people whose bags also got lost. This is when you finally realize that airline employees aren't actually thinking, "This Joe guy is really special. I'm going to make sure he gets his bag and doesn't get screwed. After all, it's *his* vacation." Next time, just bring the carry-on.

8. That site you wanted to see was under renovation.

Oh man. This is the worst. I've missed out on a museum in Paris because it was under strike. I missed a museum in Rome because it was under renovation. This is a huge bummer. Sometimes you can look it up and double-check, but sometimes you're in for a rude awakening. I should have looked this up ahead of time, but alas, I didn't. And I was rudely awoken.

9. You were sick.

You sat next to Typhoid Mary on the plane and walked away with a nasty cold. Or, you already had a cold and the plane clogged up your ears so you can't hear anything. Or maybe, you get food poisoning and the hotel doesn't have air conditioning... and it's 90 degrees. Or maybe you have to spend the week in a hospital getting your kidney stones treated. Or maybe you get an infection and you're there for two months. Every single one of these are real things that have actually happened to people I know. (I was the one with the clogged ears and actually had to pour water up my nose to try to get my ears to pop.) These things suck. And there is really no way around it. Sickness can really take the wind out of the sails.

10. The vacation just wasn't long enough.

All that travel time made you tired and by the time you felt like you could finally relax, the vacation was over. This is hard because sometimes you only have a few days for vacation and there is really nothing you can do about it. I recommend doing whatever you have to in order to get into "vacation mode." Maybe cancel your plans the day before you leave and start early. With the busy lives we live right now, getting relaxed takes time. Pretend that you're on the beach: make a Pina Colada and turn on Island music on Pandora. Don't let your vacation come and go. Do what you have to in order to prepare yourself for a relaxing time.

23

Creating an itinerary

At this stage, the most important thing is that your itinerary gives you enough detail so that you can create a good travel budget.

What you need for your itinerary:

- Where you're going
- Number of days you'll be traveling
- What you'll be doing (you don't need all the details at this stage, just a general idea)
- Driving/flying times

You can use the trip planning document (found at the end of this book) or you can create one that makes sense for you. You want one document where you're keeping track of everything in one place. You can use this to keep track of bookings, schedule, budget, etc.

Once you have the destination (or a few) selected, you can create the itinerary. This is where you need to decide how many days you'll need to complete this trip. If you already know you have a week, then that's the time frame you're going to work with. Sometimes, at this stage, I find out a week is not enough to execute the things I really want to do, aka seeing Italy, France, Spain and Germany all in one week. In that case, I may go back to my destination lists and go through the exercises again to select a destination that can be done in a shorter period of time.

Start by estimating how many days you think you'll need to accomplish the things you want to do on this trip. Look at flights to see how long it's going to take. Will it be a full day of travel or half a day of travel? Are you renting a car and driving somewhere? Write down driving times. Will you need to break up some of that travel for an overnight stay? Consider how you travel best. If you're getting in at 9 p.m., and you want to drive to another town, you may want to stay near the airport that night to avoid picking up your rental car to drive for another 3 hours. Think through what activities you want to do. Is there a place you want to hike? How long will that take? How many things do you want to squeeze into one day? Will you want to spread out the activities? This is my thought process. After I do this, I realize if the trip will be 5 days, 6 days, or 12 days. Europe is always longer because you have to account for two full travel days and jet lag. So you can't just go from one thing to another, it's just not realistic. Think these things through in your planning.

Below are two examples of itineraries I created at this stage: one domestic and one international. (You'll notice not everything is filled in yet. Once we get into planning the sightseeing, this itinerary will fill out with restaurant reservations, specific sightseeing tours, snorkeling excursions, etc.)

Itinerary Example (Domestic)

Destination: Utah
Main thing to see/do: Visit national parks
Number of days: 7
Main way to get around: Flying and driving

DATE	TIME	WHAT	NOTES/DRIVE TIMES
Fri., July 1	12:45 p.m.	Fly into Salt Lake City	
		Pick up rental car	
	2:00 p.m.	Drive to Airbnb Moab	3 hr. 45 min. drive from airport
	6:00 p.m.	Arrive in Moab	
Sat., July 2		Arches National Park	10 min. drive from Airbnb
Sun., July 3		Canyonlands National Park	35 min. ride from Airbnb
	4:00 p.m.	Drive to Cortez, Colorado	2 hrs. drive from Canyonlands
		Mesa Verde National Park	Evening drive-through
Mon., July 4	12:45 p.m.	Drive to Salt Lake City	6 hr. drive from Cortez
Tues., July		Antelope Island	1 hr. from SLC

5			
Wed., July 6		Salt Lake City sightseeing	
Thurs., July 7	7:30 a.m.	Depart Salt Lake City	

Itinerary Example (International)

Destination: London and Paris

Main thing to see/do: Museums, churches, cathedrals and monuments

Number of days: 11

Main way to get around: Flying and train

DATE	TIME	WHAT	NOTES
Day 1	4:30 pm	Depart Columbus	
Day 2	8:35 am	Arrive London	Survive jet-lag
Day 3		Day-trip to Dover and stop in Canterbury	1 hr. 40 min train ride
Day 4		Day trip to York	2 hr. train ride
Day 5		Day trip to the Cotswolds: Chipping Campen, Moreton-in-Marsh, Stow-on-the-Wold	1 hr. 40 min train ride
Day 6		Sightsee in London	
Day 7	8:00 am	Depart London	
	11:15 am	Arrive Paris	

Day 8		Sightsee in Paris	
Day 9		Day trip to Versailles	
Day 10		Sightsee in Paris	
Day 11	10:15am	Depart Paris	
	11:30am	Arrive London	
		Tube to Heathrow	
	3:00pm	Depart London	

You'll see that I had the destination in mind, and had already done some research on day-trips I wanted to do. If you're not sure of all the day-trips at this stage, that's fine. You at least need to know the city you plan to fly in and out of, and how many days you plan to be there. Now, you can begin to craft your travel budget.

Creating a travel budget

As far as packing goes, you want to plan for the best case scenario. As far as budgeting goes, you want to plan for the worst case scenario.

You want to list everything you can think of that will cost money. The last thing you want is to only prepare for the bare-bones and later find out you're $1,000 short and have to start cutting things out; like major sights or a decent meal in your favorite city. You don't want to trim things that are important, so make sure to take your time thinking about everything you'll be spending money on.

The best trick to budgeting is some trial and error. Every time I go on a trip, I keep track of every dollar I spend. This helps me in future planning. I come home and add up everything I spent on food, transportation, sightseeing, etc., and add that to the list. I have a chart that shows me what I thought I would spend vs. what I actually spent. I have done this for every trip, and now I'm pretty good at knowing realistically how much we're going to spend. In fact, on the last trip I went on, there was only a $30 difference. That meant I was within $30 of the amount I budgeted for. That's some good planning right there! The travel budget helps me not have big surprises when I'm home and find out I actually overspent $1,000! (Of course that would never happen. Is my nose growing?) If I'm going to overspend $1,000, I want to do it because I wanted to, not because I didn't plan well enough.

Things you'll want to include in your travel budget:

1. Flights
This will most likely be the largest expense, depending on the destination. For a trip overseas, it's usually the largest. This book gives some tips on how to save money on airfare, but you'll want to look at basic flights from your hometown to the city of your choice and go for a midrange price. For example, if you search and find the cheapest flight to be $515, and they go up to about $800, budget for $650 just to be safe.

2. Ground transportation
This includes your car rentals, buses, subways, taxis, bicycle rentals, metro rides, etc. How will you be getting around while you're there? And how much does it look like it's going to cost? Car rental prices are easy to price

through sites like Orbitz or Expedia. You don't have to use that site in the end, but use them to get an idea of cost. If you're not renting a car, are you using public transportation? Most public transportation outlets have websites. For an estimate, you can see how much a daily metro ride costs, and times that by the number of days you'll be there.

3. Accommodations

There are a lot of accommodation choices; we'll talk about those later. Right now, you want to have a basic idea of how much things will cost in the towns you'll be staying. Prices vary greatly, so I would do a quick search on Booking.com or Airbnb.com, to see how much the going nightly rate is. When I'm not ready to do this yet, my go-to number is $125 a night. Maybe that seems high (or maybe it seems low) but that's typically the average of what we as a couple spend per night in major European and American cities.

4. Daily food

This can be a tricky thing to guess and requires a lot of research. If you Google "how much do I need per day in _____" you'll get a lot a whole mix of answers. It's because it depends on the type of traveler you are. Budget travelers can get by on very little per day by eating only at grocery stores and markets. For those who want to eat out, they are looking at spending more. Without any research, my go-to price estimate is $10 for breakfast, $15 for lunch and $20 for dinner per person. That is a very liberal estimate, but it works if I don't have time to do all the restaurant research up front. A lot of hotels and bed and breakfasts are going to have free breakfast, so the chances of needing $10 every day for breakfast is slim.

5. Sightseeing

You can do a generic daily estimate (such as $25 a day), but I would recommend writing out all the places you'll want to go and looking up each entrance fee. Depending on the country you're going to, you could end up spending quite a bit that you might not be prepared for. For example, a ticket to the Tower of London costs 22 pounds, which is actually about $34. Those are the kinds of things you want to be prepared for. I also include any type of boat excursion (snorkeling), wine tasting tours, bike rentals, etc. Anything that you plan on doing during the day should be included in this list.

6. Shopping and miscellaneous purchases

Souvenirs, extra bottles of wine, a scarf, a bottle of water at a museum, an umbrella, you'll have things that come up and you want to have a small budget that is ready to handle a few extras. I usually keep at least $100 in this category, because you never know what will come up. When you're at a lodge and someone is selling bracelets made by members of a tribe who used beads from the jungle, you want to have money for that.

7. Guidebooks, walking shoes, travel-related items

These are things you'll purchase ahead of time, but you want to include this in your trip budget. You'll need to have good guidebooks and walking shoes. If you don't have packing cubes, a toiletry bag or a good suitcase, plan to purchase some of those items. The more I travel, the smaller this portion of the budget gets and typically only includes guidebooks. However, if I'm doing a large hiking excursion, I may have quite a bit of items on this list.

Here is an example budget from a trip I took in 2013:

Barcelona, Lisbon, Rome and Sicily

Budget: Two People

What	*Estimate Cost*	Notes	Actual
Two open jaw flights: CMH to Barcelona, Rome to CMH	*2,280*	1,140 per flight	1,493
Four round-trip flights per person, within countries	*630*	Average 40 a person with one checked bag	648
Hotels, 13 nights	*1,430*	Average 110/night	1,586
Car rental	*200*		200
Fuel for car and GPA	*125*		187
Transportation within the cities	*150*	Trains/buses	246
Food, 14 days	*700*	25/person/day Breakfast: hotels 10/lunch, 15/dinner	867
Sightseeing	*500*	35/day for two people	474
Shopping/Misc	*200*		75
Travel books	*50*	Barcelona, Lisbon, Rome and Sicily	50
Shoes (1 pair each)	*100*	Outlet mall	100
Travel items from Amazon	*50*		60
Total	*6,415*		5,986

You can see what I budgeted vs. what I actually spent. You can see I was pretty close on a lot of them. In some categories, I spent more, and in some I spent less. However, by budgeting for what I thought we would spend, we ended up spending about $430 less than I thought we would. That's $215 a person. For 14 days, that's an extra $15 per day that we didn't spend. That money could then go towards the next trip.

Ways to trim down your travel budget

Once you have an estimated budget, and you've looked at your general finances, you may notice that it is going take you some time to save for that trip. Let's say you have $150 a month to commit to saving for a trip and you see that your dream trip is going to cost $3,500. That means it is going to take two years to save for the trip. If you don't want to wait that long and/or you're willing to change a few things around, you could go on the trip sooner.

A few ways I've managed to cut down on my trip expenses have included anything from choosing another airport to cutting off a day or two from the itinerary. Here are some ways you could possibly cut down your travel expense budget.

1. Picking a different departure airport.
Are there other airports besides your home-base airport you could fly out of? Since we're in Central Ohio, Columbus is the best airport for us. However, I would consider driving to Washington, D.C. which is only 6 hours from us. I found flights to South America that were $450 cheaper, per person, leaving from there. Even with a $60 hotel, $100 for parking and $80 for gas, we'd still save $660 on airfare, which is a great deal. Another option if you're in the Midwest is driving and staying with a friend or family member who lives near a larger airport. Staying with Aunt Sally in New York might save you some $$$. (There are more details on this in the booking flights portion of the book.)

2. Picking a different arrival airport.

If your dream is to go to Paris but tickets to London are a lot cheaper, maybe consider flying to London and taking the Chunnel over. You want to do your homework because additional transportation from the place you fly in to the place you're going to could add up. But if the cost savings is significant enough, this could work for you.

3. Rearranging your itinerary.

If you're dead set on which destination you've picked, then this won't work, but if you have wiggle room, you could change some things around. I have lists of different places I want to see all the time. If airfare to one place is outrageous, I may consider waiting on that trip and going on a less expensive one. For example, airfare to South America is very expensive from where I am. If I have a trip planned in the spring for South America, but ticket prices are too expensive, I will choose a less expensive destination that I equally want to go to. Like I said, it may not be available to rearrange your itinerary. But if you're flying into one country and leaving another, you can obviously choose to start in the country with the least expensive airfare.

4. Finding cheaper hotel accommodations.

I cannot say enough good things about bed and breakfasts. What a great way to save some money on accommodations. You can forgo staying at an expensive boutique hotel, and find a great hotel with character that is half the cost. Even if you think you've found a perfect place to stay, keep looking until you find something less expensive that will work for you.

5. Planning a trip with friends to split costs.

I don't plan trips with other people so I can save some money, but if you have friends who want to go on a trip with you, you can save some money this way. Ways you can split the costs with other people include: taxi fare, car rentals, Airbnb condo, apartment rentals or the possibility of getting group-rated prices at sightseeing locations. If you drink, you can split the cost of a bottle of wine and share it together.

6. Forgoing restaurants for cheaper grocery store options.

One trip, I mapped out every place we went and marked the closest grocery stores to our hotel or B&B. I wanted to make sure we could walk to the grocery store for food to make sandwiches, snacks and breakfast. This can save a ton on a trip where you're mostly eating at restaurants with inflated prices. (This goes double if you're staying in a huge city like Rome, Paris or New York. Prices are very high.) Rick Steves talks about staying somewhere that serves breakfast and packing up some meat and a croissant for later. He figures you're paying to stay there, so you might as well get some more mileage out of the food.

7. Finding ways to do it yourself.

We had a tour scheduled with a company that was going to cost $150 a person. Instead, we found a good guide online, downloaded some maps and free audio guides and did the tour ourselves. All we had to pay for was an entrance fee, but we ended up saving about $250 total. Tours can be great, but if they're too expensive, find other ways to do it.

8. Cutting the trip length down.

Yes, I would love to go to Europe and stay for two months. However, I know that with two people, for every day we stay, we will spend roughly $150-$200 per day. By just shaving off two days, we could save $300-400 dollars on the entire trip itself.

How to save money for a trip

One of the biggest deterrents I hear from people when it comes to traveling is that they don't have any money to go on a trip. People ask me all the time *how can you afford to take those trips?*

The obvious fact is that you do need money to travel. However, you need money for everything else as well. I guarantee you spend money on something I don't because I would rather save my money for a trip. There is nothing wrong with spending your hard-earned money on what you choose to spend it on. So if you want to go on a trip, you can use money towards a trip instead of eating out three times a week. What's most important to you? Can you live without cable? If so, you can use the money you would have spent on cable to save for a long weekend trip to the beach. It's all a matter of what's important to you.

Once you decide that you'd like to go on a trip, and you've followed my tips for creating a travel budget, you know what you need to save for. Let's say you figured out you need $3,500 for a trip. Now, you can look at your home budget to see how much you can save per month. You can also look at your budget, and see ways you can cut things out. For us, food was a big area.

A lot of us know this, but consider some of the data compiled by the U.S. Department of Labor. They produced a chart called "where does all the money go?" (You can find this under Google images). It's fascinating to see how much we as U.S. consumers actually spend on things like reading, entertainment, food, alcohol, housing, tobacco, etc. We spent a lot of money on a lot of different things; some things needful and some things not-so-much.

We all make choices on what we're going to spend our money on. My husband and I have considered that traveling is something we want to do. We consider that when making decisions. For example, it's just the two of us so we don't need a huge house with five bedrooms and three bathrooms. We could afford to pay for a larger home, but that would mean that we can't do anything else. To us, that's not worth it. We would rather pay less and have a smaller home than pay more and not be able to go anywhere.

Do you need to eat out three times a week? Do you both need your own car? Do you have to have internet at your house? Do you need to buy Starbucks every day? Do you need that brand new coat, or is the one from last year sufficient? My recommendation to you is that you sit down and write out everything you spend money on. Then, go through and number each item according to its priority level. Then re-write the list in order of priorities. Take a look at those last three things on the list. Can you get rid of any of those?

Sometimes this requires thinking outside the box. Consider areas of your life that you may be throwing your money away. Instead of throwing away money on a mediocre meal from a chain restaurant, put it toward going snorkeling in the Caribbean!

Here are a few things we've done to cut out needless spending, to make some room for travel savings:

1. Not buying more groceries until we eat everything we had.
That sounds like a no brainer, but we often will go buy more food if we're craving something, instead of just eating whatever we have until it's gone. There was a whole two weeks where we decided we wouldn't buy anything, we would just eat what we had. You'd be surprised how much food is actually in your cabinets that just sit there. We made a crock pot of soup and put all the canned veggies and beans we could find. We used up every bag and box of rice and noodles that we'd been storing. We made muffins from a mix we had, we had oatmeal for breakfast. We literally ate everything. I challenge you to try this and let your creative side come out and see what you can make with what you have. (This is actually fun even if you're not trying to save money.)

2. Pack your lunch or go home for lunch.
When I have the ability to go home for lunch, I always do. My husband is a little further away and used to buy lunch at least 2-3 times a week. This was mostly because it was easier. Now, we opt to pack the majority of the time. This also saves money because you end up eating ALL the leftovers.

3. Forgoing restaurants, or going for cheaper options.

Not only does it pack on the calories (and thus expanding your waistline) but it's also a money suck to eat out for all your meals. For two people to go out, you're looking at $30-$40 for one meal. You could get four chicken breasts, a 5 lb bag of potatoes and ingredients for a salad for less than half of that. And you would have enough for leftovers. By just cutting out one meal eating out a week, you could potentially save yourself $100 a month. That's $100 you can put towards a trip.

Instead of each ordering a giant meal, try sharing a meal. Some of those portions are insane. Last time we went out, we spent $15 for the two of us. We shared a meal and each ordered water. Yeah, we weren't stuffed to the brim, but we were content.

4. Going to the thrift store first, before buying something brand new.

I have always been a thrifter, because I love vintage things. But if I need something like a picture frame, a kitchen utensil or a household item, you can often find quality items for really inexpensive. A lot of my favorite kitchen pieces, like a crystal creamer, I bought from a thrift store for less than $2. I have found brand new pots, pans and hand towels at the thrift store, too. I also got a small table for our living room that had already been repainted for $10. Always go there to see if you can find something before dropping $50-$100 at the store for the same thing.

5. Acquiring hand-me-downs.

I've hosted a clothing exchange party and a home goods exchange. In a nut shell, people bring things they don't need or use anymore and everyone looks through the items brought and takes what they would like. At the clothing party, I got a great jacket I could use for travel. At the home goods party, I got a great a great set of new pans. A lot of us have things we don't use lying around that we can give away. If we need something, maybe someone else has it so you don't have to go buy it.

6. Keeping the thermostat at livable (not always comfortable) temperatures.

When I tell this to people, I usually get the stare-down. It's like I've suggested they forgo eating. Everyone likes the idea of having every comfort available to them. However, my grandmother lived for YEARS without an air-conditioning unit. It is possible to live with a little extra heat in the summer and some colder breezes in the winter. So maybe this means drinking a few more ice-cold drinks in the summer to keep cool, or putting on an extra sweater to stay warm in the winter. It's not going to kill you. It hasn't killed me yet.

These are just some of the ways we've managed to trim the budget. I'm not saying you have to give up everything. But I am saying you probably have a lot of waste that you're not even thinking about. Start thinking about your own budget and ways you could cut some things out to save money for a trip.

A little bit goes a long way: how you can use those small savings to plan a trip

So you went through your budget and found waste. I told you that you'd find some! You decided to eat lunches at home, not buy a new couch and live with some cooler temperatures in the winter. You're now able to save $80 a month to put towards travel. You're not ready to go on your big dream trip yet; you just want to do a small little get away. So let's see how much we can stretch that $80.

You've saved $80 a month for 4.25 months. You now have $340. Let's start with Kayak explore and see if I could plan a trip for $340. After looking at the explore option, I saw that I could fly to Los Angeles, Utah, Texas, Florida or Colorado for $340 or less. For this example, I'm going to choose somewhere I've never been, that's less than $340 so I can see how far I can get on a trip with it. Obviously, I can't spend all the money on the flight, but it was a good exercise to see how far I could get for $340.

Since I've never been to Columbia, South Carolina, and tickets are $170, I'm going to go there. So I've chosen to go there on a two-day trip. I can fly out on a Tuesday at 6 a.m., which gets me in at 9:30 a.m., and then come back the following day, leaving at 6 p.m. and coming back at 10:30 p.m.

They have public transportation (The Comet) from the airport to the downtown area, only $1.50 one way, or $3 for the whole day.

I found a room on Airbnb for $105 a night. There were places for half that price, but this place was right in the middle of the downtown area, which would enable me to walk and not have to rent a car.

What will I do when I'm there? Well, within walking distance, I can visit a few free historical sites or museums:

- The McKissick Museum, part of the University of South Carolina, and has many exhibitions on display.
- The South Carolina State House, which offers free guided walking tours Monday through Friday.
- I can also walk to the Columbia Canal and Riverfront Park for a little stroll.

I have $62 left for food after I bought my flight, my room and $3 for bus transportation. There are restaurants nearby that look inexpensive, according to a map on TripAdvisor.

A two-day trip to Columbia South Carolina:

$170 flight

$3 ground transportation

$105 Airbnb room

$0 Entertainment

$62 food

Total: $340

This was so much fun, let's do one more. I've been here dozens of times, but it's a fun, vibrant city that I always want to go back to: Washington, D.C. Our money will go far here because all the Smithsonian Museums are free.

For those same dates (April 21-22) I can fly to D.C. for $175. The flight leaves at 8 a.m. and gets in at 9:15 a.m. I fly out the next day at 10 p.m. and get in at 11:30 p.m. The metro system costs $2.35 from the airport to the main part of the city.

I found an Airbnb room for $97, and it's blocks from the metro, near the National Mall. (About a 20 minute metro ride to the Washington Monument.) This means I can walk everywhere, and will only need the metro when I go to and from the airport. I found a TripAdvisor Guide that lists all the things you can do and see, and most of them are free.
The Eastern Market, is open from 7 a.m. to 7 p.m., and looks like they have good inexpensive lunch options.

A two-day trip to Washington D.C.:

$175 flight

$5 ground transportation

$97 Air bnb room

$0 Entertainment

$63 food

Total: $340

Not a bad way to spend $340, am I right?

A little bit goes a long way: how you can use those small savings to plan a trip

Couples Edition

The last edition was for a solo trip. Let's say there are two of you that want to go on a trip. You looked around your budget and found the following things you could cut out:

- Dining out two times a month at ($25 each)
- One trip to the movies ($22)
- One trip to get ice cream ($8)
- One trip to Starbucks ($6)
- Buying one new clothing item ($24)
- Buying unnecessary things at Target when bored ($40)
- Two bottles of wine ($10 each)
- Four fast food meals ($28)
- Buying one new unnecessary household item ($50)
- One impulse grocery store item ($7)

That totals $250. Now, you probably will eat out once in a while, and have to buy something needful. So let's just say between all that waste, you decide you could get away with saving $100 towards travel, and just using $150 for those "incidentals."

Side note, if you looked at your budget and didn't find things like that, you didn't look hard enough. Print off your bank statements and highlight everything you *really* didn't need. You should do this once in your life anyways, so why not now?

So we've saved $100 from January to September and we have $900. Where will we go? Using the Kayak explore option, we can price some flights. There is a flight from Columbus to Boston that we'd fly in on a Friday and leave on a Sunday. Tickets are $256 a person. So $512 for flights, only leaves us $388 for everything else.

I found a beautiful, roof deck apartment on Airbnb, in the heart of Boston, for $125 a night. Total would be $280 with fees. That leaves us $108 for two days of food, which I believe is doable. Since we have our own place with a full kitchen, we can purchase some meals at the grocery store and cook ourselves. We can pack sandwiches, and fruit and snacks.

There are also plenty of free things to do in Boston, there is water, great history, and unique architecture. I found multiple blog posts that list free things to do in Boston, including walking tours!

```
┌─────────────────────────────────────────────────┐
│         Three day trip to Boston, for a couple:   │
│                 Two flights $512                  │
│                  Lodging $280                     │
│                    Food $108                      │
│                  **Total $900**                   │
└─────────────────────────────────────────────────┘
```

So maybe we're not feeling a big city scene, but want something with nature or the ocean. How about we see how far we can get in Florida? There are flights to Fort Myers in September for $230 a ticket. One flight leaves 6 a.m. and gets in at 10:20 a.m on a Saturday. The departure flight leaves at 7 p.m. which gets us back into Columbus at 11:15 p.m on a Monday. This means we basically have three days in Florida, but only have to pay for two nights lodging.

I found an awesome Airbnb place that's in Naples, Florida, that's within walking distance to the beach, restaurants and shopping. The place is $222 for two nights. It also has free use of beach chairs and bicycles, which is a money-saving and activity-boosting bonus. E-Z Rent-a-car is $86, and that will ensure that we can get from the airport to Naples and around the beach. I would estimate that we'd need about $8 in fuel to and from the airport, and around the beach. So I'll estimate about $15, and to round it out we'll say $100 for car and fuel.

That leaves $118 for food for two people for three days. That's not a ton, but since we're renting a place that has a kitchen, we can easily get away with buying some groceries and making our own food to take to the beach. Since we're renting a car, we can go to Sanibel Island and do some seashell hunting. I had no idea that these beaches were lined with shells, and I can't tell you how excited I am to go on this fake trip. Hunting for beach loot is my favorite thing to do at the beach.

Three-day trip to Naples, Florida, for a couple:
Two flights $460
Lodging $222
Food $118
Car rental and fuel $100
Total $900

The beauty about this is hopefully you were saving money by simply not buying things you don't need so you can go somewhere fun. For a much longer trip somewhere that you really want to go, obviously it's worth it to save as long as it takes to be able to do that. But if you know you want to just take a weekend to go somewhere other than your hometown, there are other ways to do that for cheap. Of course, you can always drive places. There are plenty many places within 10 hours driving that you spend the weekend, and save yourself even more money. There are many possibilities.

A little bit goes a long way: how you can use those small savings to plan a trip

International Edition

If you're not satisfied with a quick weekend trip, and if you don't think you can actually afford to go to another country, let's talk about this. Many people choose to go on cruises because they're inexpensive ways to see many places. If you aren't a cruise-person, then read on.

I have chosen to plan an international trip for $2,400 because I know that the median household income in Ohio is $46,093, and I'm sure that's based on the fact that many families in Ohio have two incomes. So let's say that you have $46,093 per year. After taking out 25 percent for taxes, that's $34,569 a year. That equates to $2,880 a month. Experts say that you should be spending about 1/3 of your income on housing so that would be $865. I would estimate about $300 for utilities. Let's say you have two $200 car payments, you spend $150 a week on groceries and fuel, you have a $120 a month cell bill. That still leaves $595 for whatever other bills you have to pay. I am guessing there's at least $200 in there you could save towards travel.

I'm a pretty practical person and I don't believe in planning trips that you never intend to go on. I know that it may seem like you don't have any money to save toward travel, but hopefully thinking through ways you waste money or spend money on things you don't need, you will find out that you actually do have some money to put towards travel. Maybe you can't afford to save $200 a month. Maybe you can afford $100 and can use some of a tax return towards a trip. There are ways to do it, if you plan and think it through.

I've started again with our Kayak explore options. I found that I can get a flight to Cozumel for $393 a person in May for two people. After airfare, we're left with $1,614 for a week. I found a place on Airbnb, it's in a great location and looks clean and comfortable. For a week, it costs $521. It's a 20 minute walk to the beach or downtown, it's close to two grocery stores (one right around the corner) and a 5-10 minute walk from the airport.

Although we don't necessarily need a car, if we want to visit any of the Mayan ruins, it would be a lot easier and give us more flexibility for sightseeing. I found a car rental for $152 for a week, and I would estimate about $40 for fuel, so that's $192.

After flights, a place to stay and a rental car, we have $901 left for sightseeing and food. I've taken a look at some of the prices in one of their grocery stores, and prices seem very reasonable (even on the inexpensive side.) Restaurants don't look over the top either, so I think we can budget $30 for food per day, per person. That is $420. After food, flights, a rental car, and a place to stay, we still have $481.

Cozumel to Playa del Carmen ferry costs about $23 a person. Playa del Carmen has lots of activities that seem very reasonably priced. From here, you can book a tour of the Chichen Itza. I found one tour for $95 a person. Other options include Ek Balam Mayan Ruins, Yal ku Lagoon, and Cenote Canaak Tun.

You can use your $481 however you want, you can book a few snorkeling tours, visit some ruins, have a nice fancy dinner, or even stop by a market and get some loot to take home with you. You probably wouldn't even need to spend all that. After looking at fees and tour costs, I would estimate that $300 should be sufficient for two people to enjoy some good activities. (For example, snorkeling in Yal ku Lagoon is only $10 a person for snorkel gear, and entrance to Ek Balam is only $10 a person.)

It seems that Mexico is a great get-away for a good price.

```
┌─────────────────────────────────────────────────┐
│         Seven-day trip to Cozumel, for a couple:  │
│                  Two flights $786                 │
│                  Lodging $521                     │
│             Car rental and fuel: $192             │
│                   Food $420                       │
│                Sightseeing: $300                  │
│                 Total $2,219                      │
└─────────────────────────────────────────────────┘
```

For an international trip, this is pretty good. We even came in under
budget!

How about a non-beach destination for you mountain junkies? Let's see
how far we can get in Canada for $2,400. Tickets to Vancouver are $423,
for June 2-9. (7 whole days!) Canada is going to be more expensive than
Mexico, for sure, but I think we can still pull something off. Plane tickets
are $846, leaving us $1,554 for everything else.

Since we have an entire week, I think two nights in the city would be good
to start, and then we'll see if we can venture off to somewhere with more
nature. I found a place on Airbnb with a private balcony off the bedroom,
which I think is wonderful. (It's only $58 a night, and is a close walk to
public transportation.)

There are a lot of free things to do in Vancouver. I found a National
Geographic Guide with a lot of ideas that includes lots of outdoor places
like Granville Island, Canada Place and Stanley park, as well as a cathedral
and an observatory.

Vancouver Island nearby boasts great seascapes and parks and through word-of-mouth I've heard Tofino is one of the most beautiful beaches in the world. I think this might be a good place to spend a few days relaxing. We can pick up a rental car for this excursion and have it from Thursday through Monday. The rental car is $100, and I'm estimating $100 for fuel. (Since Tofino is 350 miles roundtrip.)

I found a gorgeous home on Airbnb that is perched on a hill with water views for $97 a night. We'll stay here four nights which equates to $387. There is so much to do near Tofino, and with a rental car we have the ability to travel around and see it. There's kayaking, wind-surfing, many parks including Pacific Rim National Park.

Food looks a little on the pricey side in Canada, so for two people, I would estimate $40/day per person. I would also give yourself about $150 for sightseeing adventures, maybe a Kayak rental and park fees, if they apply.

Seven-day trip to Vancouver, for a couple:

Two flights: $846

Three nights in Vancouver: $174

Four nights in Tofino: $387

Car rental and fuel: $200

Food $560

Sightseeing and park entrances: $150

Transportation within the city, and miscellaneous: $75

Total $2,392

There you have it. Now, stop telling yourself you don't have money to go anywhere. I challenge you to do the same thing. See how much waste you have in your budget, save a few bucks here and there, and see what you can come up with. I was surprised how far I could get with $80-$100 a month. I hope you're able to find some great ways to stretch your savings.

Booking the trip

Now that you selected a destination, created an itinerary and a budget, you're ready to actually start booking things. At this stage, I always get a little nervous. Purchasing $1,500 airline flights can be slightly nerve-racking; especially if you're not sure you are getting the best deal. Even though the nerves may kick in at this point, you are able to book this stuff. You are your own travel agent, after all, and you are going to do the very best research to get the very best deals. Once you've done that, you really are ready to punch in your credit card numbers and start charging.

In this section, we'll discuss the following:

- How to use TripAdvisor (the "Wikipedia" of traveling sites)
- Finding and booking airfare (and tips for getting the best deal)
- Finding and booking accommodations
- How to avoid false advertising
- Tips for finding free things to do

How to use TripAdvisor

TripAdvisor is one of my favorite travel-related sites. It's kind of the "Wikipedia" of traveling, in that the reviews are written by people like you and me. It's a place to see the actual photographs of a hotel or place taken by real customers, not just the company itself. It has all the information about the top destinations, sites, cities, beaches, hotels, and more. Not everything on it will be trustworthy, and not everything on it will be useful. However, it is a great tool for gathering lots of information for your next trip.

I think the best feature it has are the reviews. As people review a place, they are sorted from the best to the worst. If you select "hotels" the best-rated ones will show up first. In order to write a review, you have to have a profile. This profile allows other travelers to see your age and find out what type of traveler you are. Therefore, if they're writing a review about a hotel and they gave it a low grade, you can find out the kind of expectations they have. (ie. if they are a luxury traveler, and they gave a low rating to a budget hotel, you can deduce that it might not be a bad hotel, but just not their "cup of tea.") You're not allowed to post anything of self-promotion or links to yourself as a travel agent. It's just for honest reviews from people who have visited the location. It's simple to use, and extremely helpful.

If you don't have a profile, you should create one. That way you can write reviews and keep track of all the wonderful places you've visited on your personal travel map. Now you're ready to use TA. Let's pick a destination and go through some of the lesser known features.

As an example, go to the TripAdvisor website, and type in "Barcelona."

It's pretty self-explanatory, but each header will bring you to look at hotels, attractions or restaurants. One thing you may not have noticed is that last box that says "Travel Guides." Not every city will have Travel Guides, but those that do can give you some great insider information that you may not have known otherwise.

One of the travel guides is called "Barcelona Off the beaten path." In here, there is a recommendation to visit one of the parks there. And under that park are the following tips:

- Guided tours are available with a reservation.
- The best way to get here is by metro. Take the green line L3 to Mundet, and from there it is a 10 minute walk.
- There is an entrance fee, but if you visit on a Wednesday or Sunday it´s free.

This is quality information that you may not have known otherwise. So be sure to scroll through the different guides and see if any one peaks your interest.

Did you know you can see prices of hotels right from TA? Enter your dates of travel through the hotel tab and then you can see the highest rated hotels and their prices all the way down. You can book directly through Booking.com, Orbitz or Expedia. (Depending on which sites the hotel is listed on.)
I really like this feature because I'm always looking for the best deal on the best hotel. I also want to see what I'm getting myself into before I actually book it through a third-party website. I can read reviews and see

actual photographs of the hotel. If I just went directly to Booking.com, for example, I would only see the hotel's stock photographs, which might not be accurate.

At the top of the website, there is a "Best of 2014." This lists the top-rated destinations by country or by the world. There are also other "best ofs" including "best beaches," "best islands," and "best restaurants. If you're not sure where you want to go, this can give you some great ideas. Travelers share why that destination is a winner in their book.

Did you know you can directly message someone who wrote a review? This has proven to me to be extremely helpful to me. Yes, there are forums on TA where you can post a question and hope someone answers. But if you see that someone just stayed at a hotel where you want to stay, and you have questions about something very specific, you can message them directly and they can respond to you through your TA inbox. (Another reason why having a profile is helpful.)

Simply click on their name and under there you can see what kind of reviews they've given, and you can click the "Message" part to send them a direct message. It also gives you details about what kind of traveler they are. If they seem to match your profile, then they're a similar traveler to you. The more similar a traveler to you, the more their reviews should line up with how you would feel about a place as well. I've asked people questions about how to get to certain places, if it was over-crowded, what the neighborhood was like, etc.

TA maps are very helpful to finding out where the hotel is in relation to the top sites and restaurants. If you're considering a hotel and want to know if you'll have to walk ten miles to the site, look to the right hand side of the hotel you're reviewing and click the map under "Browse nearby." The map allows you to browse where the restaurants and sites are and where other hotels are located. As you zoom in, you can click on a place and go directly to it to see other reviews on TA.

Booking airfare

Airfare. It's the most expensive part of any trip. This means, I'm always scouring the internet looking for ways to save money on airfare. There are a lot of articles out there about travel hacks that offer tips to save money. However, some of these "travel hacks" appear a little too sketchy for my taste.

For example, one hack I read was to get a credit card with rewards, buy a gift card, then use the gift card to purchase a money order, then deposit the money order into the bank and use it to pay off the credit card. I guess technically it's not *illegal*. Maybe it's just "scamming the scammer." However, I just want to get a good deal on a plane ticket; not take a gateway drug to becoming a real money launderer.

I have had success with some of these tips to saving money on airfare, and I have listed them here.

1. Purchase your tickets on Tuesday, Wednesday or Thursday

Buying tickets in the middle of the week is the best time to buy. A lot of sources I've read agree that airlines actually drop their prices on Tuesdays in order to increase airfare purchasing. So it's proven to be one of the best times to buy tickets.

2. Set up price alerts

Sites like Kayak allow you to set up a price alert that can either email you daily or weekly with price updates. You can set the dates, and add that you're flexible in case there are deals around the time you want to fly that can save you $$. Another thing you can do is give it a max amount you want to spend. We set up a price alert when we flew to Barcelona in 2013, and tickets were around $900-$1,000. One day we got an email and the price had dropped to about $600 a ticket. We bought that day and nearly saved $800 total on airfare.

3. Purchase your tickets in the right window of time

The best time to buy overseas flights is 4-6 months out. The best time to buy a domestic ticket is about 2-3 months out. My recommendation is to set up price alerts and continue checking how much a flight costs. Then plan on purchasing during these sweet spots. In my experience, the price stays relatively the same until these windows of time and then they go up and down a bit before staying up and continue to go up. Plan on purchasing in this window of time. The absolute worst time to buy tickets is last minute. So even if you pay $50 more for purchasing the ticket two weeks early, at least don't wait so long that you end up paying $500 more.

4. Clear your browsers

According to some sources, websites look at browsing history to see if you're interested in a certain flight. Then they boost up the prices right before you're about to purchase. I'm not entirely sure this is true, but just in case... you better just clear your cookies and recent history in order to avoid inflated costs on your computer.

5. Try departing out of another airport

I'm going to spend some time explaining this one, because I think it can really pay off in the long-run. I started a Kayak alert for my destination, and the tickets were outrageous. I'm talking $1,200-$1,500 a person. However, as I started examining all of the places that I would have a layover in, I noticed a pattern. There was one layover city that came up almost every time, across all airlines. Depending on your destination, the layover pattern may be completely different. So I started playing around, and seeing patterns with any destination I plugged in. For example, if you're flying from here to many of the cities in South America, your layover will be in Atlanta. This means, that if you can find a cheaper flight to Atlanta or plan to drive there, you can possibly save a ton of money.

The destination we were looking at had all the layovers in Toronto. Toronto is only 6.5 hours from us, and makes a great hub for international travel. Here's the best part about this. Like I said, tickets were outrageous. The flight I wanted was $1,250 a person, from Columbus. Flying directly from Toronto, however, it was $675. This means that we saved $575 a ticket, just by flying out of Toronto. What will we do with our car you ask? Good question. There are actually plenty of hotels that let you rent a room and park for up to two weeks for free, or there are hotels that let you just pay for parking. I found a website called ParkSleepFly that lets you search any destination and gives you options for (big surprise here) parking, sleeping and flying. You can search for hotel and parking only, or parking only. I found parking (without hotel) for as little as $7 a day, which considering how much we're saving on airfare, is chump change. So if you include gas and parking (and potentially a hotel room), we're looking at $30 roundtrip fuel, $110 for hotel and parking. So saving $1,150 on airfare, but spending $140, means a real savings of just over $1,000. Not bad at all.

I tried out a few more, just to test my theory. This was a fun experiment. Here were my findings, from least savings to greatest savings:

- Flight from Columbus to Bahamas with a layover in Philadelphia: $510. Same dates flight from Philadelphia: $385. Drive time to Philadelphia: 7 hours, **flight savings: $125**.
- Flight from Columbus to Portland, with a layover in Chicago: $625. Same dates flight from Chicago: $425. Drive time to Chicago 5.5 hours, **flight savings: $200**
- Flight from Columbus to Dublin, with a layover in Washington, D.C. (or Chicago) $885. Same dates flight from DC: $500. Drive time to DC: 6.5 hours, **flight savings $385**
- Flight from Columbus to Tokyo, with a layover in Toronto: $1,050. Same dates flight from Toronto: $570. Drive time to Toronto: 6.5 hours, **flight savings: $480**

- Flight from Columbus to Paris, with a layover in Chicago: $1,110. Same dates flight from Chicago: $475. Drive time to Chicago: 5.5 hours, **flight savings $635**.
- Flight from Columbus to Taipei, Taiwan, with a layover in Toronto: $1,190. Same dates flight from Toronto: $520. Drive time to Toronto: 6.5 hours, **flight savings: $670**
- Flight from Columbus to Lima, Peru, with a layover in NYC: $1,195. Same dates flight from NYC: $495. Drive time to NYC: 8 hours, **flight savings $700**

As you can see, it pays to check out where those layovers are going, and see how much you might be able to save with a little bit of driving. Honestly, if you think about it, you're spending about the same amount of time you would driving to the airport, waiting and having a layover as you would just driving to the airport. 5-6 hours in the car, compared with a 2-hour flight, plus waiting time and getting to the airport in time on either side. So you're saving money, and not necessarily compromising on time. Seems like a win-win situation!

Once you've found the best deal on the internet, you're ready to book. I have booked through third-party sites, but most of the time, I book directly through the airline. If you found the price alert on Kayak, then it should take you to the actual site to book. Then it's a matter of filling in all your personal information and credit card information. I like to use a card that gets me double travel points, so that I can use those points to save on airfare down the road.

Booking accommodations

There are a lot of sites to choose from when booking accommodations. There are some that I prefer more than others, and I have reasons why. There are a lot of sites like Orbitz, Expedia, Booking.com, Hotwire, Travelocity, etc. There are also a number of vacation rental sites such as Homeaway.com, Airbnb, and even booking through TripAdvisor. There are pros and cons to each, and those are discussed in the next section. However, there are ones I prefer and use them on a more regular basis.

For hotels and bed and breakfasts, I prefer to book through Booking.com. Here are my main reasons why:

1. You pay when you get there.

Almost always you don't have to pay until you arrive. There is no down-payment or money you have to put upfront.

2. Free cancellation.

Most of the time, I can get a room that I can cancel within 48 hours of arrival. (Sometimes even 24 hours prior to arrival.) This gives me ease in booking things well in advance, and if things change I just cancel my reservation with no penalties. Booking.com has a lot of the smaller bed and breakfasts listed as well, instead of just the larger hotel chains which tend to flood sites like Expedia and Orbitz.

3. You can book as a link through TripAdvisor.

If I'm looking at hotels through TripAdvisor and I put in my dates, it gives me options on which sites I can book through. Some hotels are listed on Orbitz, Expedia and Booking.com, some are only available through the hotel website.

4. Customer service.

I booked a hotel in Edinburgh months in advance. Unfortunately, the hotel canceled our reservation on account of "being full" a day before we were supposed to be there. Booking.com offered a few other places to stay at, but they didn't have good reviews. I chose another place and then wrote a letter of complaint to them. They refunded us $50 for the extra cost to stay in another hotel. They credited our bank account quickly, which I appreciated. Even though that happened, I still felt that this site did due diligence to try and make things right.

For home rentals, I prefer Airbnb over some of the other sites. Here is why:

1. Better options.

Frankly, you get better options on Airbnb. Some of the home rental sites are specific to vacation rentals and seem more commercial. Airbnb has regular people renting out spaces in their homes, on their farms, in their tree houses, etc. You can find unique accommodation that you might not find anywhere else. Some of these places you may be hard pressed to find without this type of site.

2. Lower prices.

Their prices are overall better. If you're looking for a budget option, Airbnb is going to have more options than you would find on a vacation rental site. Some of the vacation rental options I've seen are the same as staying in a really nice Hampton Inn. If I wanted to pay $200 a night to stay somewhere, I'd stay at a hotel that changes my sheets and makes my breakfast. I don't mind making my own breakfast if I only have to pay $75 a night.

3. Review system.

Not only do you get to review the places you've stayed, but they review you as well. Instead of them just allowing anyone to stay in their home, they can see that I've had some reviewers say that I left their place clean and was a good guest in their home. This keeps honesty between the renters and the clients which I think is a good system.

Pros and cons of accommodation choices

Depending on where you are going and what type of traveler you are, you may find yourself weighing the different types of accommodations available for your trip. I'm a huge fan of Airbnb, but there are certainly times when I'd opt for a hotel instead. Bed and breakfasts are some of the best ways to see Europe, and I would certainly rather stay somewhere with a local host, then in some characterless building with a block of hotel rooms.

So how would I make the tough decision, you ask? Allow me to explain the pros and cons (as I see it) for three accommodation choices: vacation rental homes (aka Airbnb), hotels and bed and breakfasts.

Vacation rental homes (aka Airbnb)

Perfect for: uniqueness, cooking yourself, off-the-beaten path, traveling in groups, budget accommodations, local host recommendations

Drawbacks: house chores and rules, no late-night bites at the hotel restaurant, shuttle services, have to pay 100% up-front (some have very strict cancellation rules so you may not be able to get a refund if your travel plans change)

Don't be deceived by the name "bnb" in Airbnb, because it usually doesn't mean it's a bed and breakfast. Usually what it means is that you're staying either in a vacation home all on your own, or you're staying in a room or partial apartment on someone's property. There are all kinds of homes you can find on the site, but I have booked entire homes for private use.

You can certainly find unique places when you opt for Airbnb. For example, we stayed on a river in Miami with access to kayaks and an urban farm. We cooked all our meals there (saving on some $) and the cost was certainly cheaper than if we'd stayed in a hotel. We also, however, have spent more on an Airbnb, than we would have on a hotel because we were able to stay in a cottage on a working ranch in Moab. So we had a unique setting that we wouldn't have any other time.

If I'm traveling with another couple or family, almost always a full vacation home is the perfect option. You have the entire home, everyone can have a room to themselves, and it is way more cost effective than purchasing multiple hotel rooms.

However, you do have a lot more rules and chores associated with renting out someone's home. Sometimes it means an extra hour in the morning taking out the trash, doing the dishes, making the beds, etc. You also don't have a hotel bar or restaurant where you can grab a quick bite or a vending machine for a snack. You are basically on your own in that arena!

Hotel

Perfect for: convenience, hotel services (housekeeping, pools/hot tubs, access to luxuries), paying later, cancellation policy, traveling solo or as a couple

Drawbacks: cookie-cutter style rooms, more expensive, traveling in groups, no cooking facilities

If my travel plans are up-in-the-air, I will almost always opt to book a room on Booking.com (or a similar site that lets me cancel last minute for free). I'd rather have the option of cancellation, and paying when I get there, as opposed to paying up front and hoping the place I want doesn't have a strict cancellation policy.

I like hotels when I want to not have to think about meeting up with a host and getting the key; I just want to come and go as I please, without having to clean up after myself. Usually (there are always exceptions)

hotels are good locations for restaurants and sightseeing, and make it more convenient for staying in large cities. If I'm flying into a city and not renting a car, having a hotel shuttle service and access to public transportation is key, which make hotels typically the better option.

Staying in a hotel, however, is usually more expensive and I won't be able to cook my own meals, which means I'll be spending more eating at restaurants. Of course, you can always brown bag it and use the tiny fridge for a thing of mustard or mayo, but cooking a steak isn't an option in a hotel.

Bed and Breakfasts

Perfect for: international travel, costs-savings, uniqueness, meeting new people

Drawbacks: staying in close quarters with others, possibly sharing bathrooms, public transportation is difficult

If I'm traveling somewhere I don't speak the language, it's very important for me to stay somewhere with a local host who speaks English. That way I can ask navigation questions, and get suggestions for English tours or other things I might need. Sure, hotels have that, but I like to "travel like a local" and it's challenging when you are in a small town or a place that's rural to find people who speak English to ask questions. So having a host that can help is key!

I've also had some of the best breakfasts ever at these little places. Many of the b&bs where we stayed in the UK had a menu with all sorts of options for us to pick and choose. One b&b in Ecuador actually had a teenage boy deliver fresh bread on his bicycle every morning, and we watched the cook go into the courtyard to pick some fruit to juice (talk about fresh!) It's hard to beat the type of breakfast experience you'll have at a small b&b. Plus, you get to eat in a room with just a few tables of other travelers, and it's fun to meet new people and share stories.

However, some of the small b&bs have few bathrooms, and you may be waiting an hour in the morning to take a shower if you don't wake up early enough. Some of these places are also in neighborhoods and places not directly in the city, so you may be walking further or having to deal with more transportation issues than if you stayed somewhere more centrally-located. Of course there are some b&bs centrally located, but they also tend to be pricier and more "hotel-like."

How to spot false travel advertising

I see this stuff all the time. A photograph for an amazing adventure tour, an ad for a 5-star hotel that looks almost too good to be true, and a historic site that looks like it was created for stock photography. I like to call these "false advertisements", because they're misleading. They're not the real deal, the authentic deal... or anything you're looking for. But it looks like it is.

That adventure tour is twice as expensive as others, and they've paid good money for you to see the ad. The tour charges you for things that would ordinarily be free. The photographs taken of that hotel were taken when it was first built... 10 years ago. You know, before thousands of tourists have run it down. That stock photograph of the historic site was taken at the right moment, with a $4,000 camera. You can make anything look appealing with a little Photoshop and the right camera angle.

So what do you do? How do you know if what you're seeing is what you're going to get? Here are a few of my personal tips for spotting a fake experience, hotel or site.

1. Google tells me.
Google lets me know by putting a little green box with the word "ad" next to a website. It's subtle, and honestly, sometimes I still click them without even noticing. Once you click on it, you quickly see that the website is filled with advertising.

2. The website gives no substantial information or it's a third-party.

One sure give away that it's a rip off is when there is a bullet list of vague promises they make to you, with no real substantial information other than "you'll save money!" There are no links to social media with reviews, no information on the company, etc. Another thing to look for are third party websites with lists of "discounted tours", that make you unsure of what company you're actually booking with. If it's telling me I'll save $, but I actually don't even know how much a tour should cost to begin with, then it's not really saving me money. I also don't know if the company that I'm going with has good reviews. (Also take note of odd, vague "rewards" such as "Top 100 Travel Sites." I wonder who gave them these awards?)

A couple of things you'll notice right away with a legitimate website is that you can read reviews and see the costs. The website also provides links for social media and photographs. You should be able to find an "about us" section with critical information about the company, its board of directors, dates when it was founded, etc. Those are important aspects to ensure the site is legitimate.

3. I found the hotel on a third-party website.

I love Booking.com and recommend it. However, I don't use exclusively. The pictures they post are from the hotel, not from users. I recommend checking a blog review or TripAdvisor to see actual photographs of the hotel that are recent. TripAdvisor has a great feature that lets you search for hotels and then book through the third-party website, like Orbitz, Expedia or Booking.com. So I recommend never starting with the third-party website to do your research. You want to see photographs and reviews from real people first (as I mentioned in the "how to use TripAdvisor" section).

4. I'm looking at stock photographs and not photographs taken from real customers.

I love perusing Google images, but I also know that the best, most doctored photographs tend to be at the top of the list. However, I want to see the real un-doctored ones, so I have a better idea of what I'm actually going to see. You have to do some more searching and digging to find the real reviews with actual traveler photographs. If you Google search Cancun beach, you'll see some beautiful photographs. Some even say "wallpaper" on them. But is that really the beach I'm actually going to see? There are no people or garbage; everything is perfect. It would be naive to think that's the beach I'm going to. So, search for some blog reviews. I found quite a few for Cancun that include honest reviews from a person with photographs that are more realistic. You can see if that's really what you want to see, or if "meh.. looks like every other beach!"

Make sure to always dig a little deeper to make sure you're getting what you want. If it looks too good to be true, maybe it is. Some places are gorgeous, amazing and you can't believe you found it! But you want to be sure, so do the extra homework to find out.

Sightseeing: things that are free

Traveling costs money. No way around that. But, there are so many things that are free about travel that you shouldn't take for granted. Yes, you have to pay for food. Yes, you have to pay for a place to stay. However, there are so many things that cost you $0.

I've mentioned this before, but getting out and exploring is just as much "traveling" as flying to Paris. Maybe not as exotic and dreamy, but you don't have to shell out thousands of dollars to enjoy exploring, especially when you consider all the free things available to travelers.

1. Audio guides and walking tours.
Many cities offer free audio guides and walking tours. (Ahem, we offer one in my hometown that I worked on!) You can almost always find a free

tour (or downloadable app) that takes you to some unique, off-the-beaten-track places. For example, Chicago Walking Tours offer Free Tours by Foot. (Tips are encouraged, but not required.) A lot of free audio guide apps are available to download for some National Parks, such as one in Death Valley. It pays to do a little research on the place you're going to see what downloads or walking tours are available. (Pun intended.)

2. Admission to some zoos, museums and parks. There is almost always some free admission to attractions in any city or country. For example, in one of the most expensive cities to visit, London, you can see most of the greatest museums for free: British Library, National Gallery, British Museum, etc. All of the monuments and Smithsonian Museums are free in Washington D.C. (perks of our taxes already paying for them). St. Louis Zoo and the Smithsonian National Zoo in D.C. are free as well. Additionally, many cities that require you to pay for admission offer free admission days. When we visited Lisbon, we museum-hopped on Sunday and enjoyed free admission to all the major sites. Some museums may have a certain day or time that offers free admission, so even if you think it costs money, check their website. You may be able to work your schedule around so you can visit free-of-charge! Although our National Parks aren't free (they're not expensive, but they're not free), there are many local city and state parks that are free.

Visiting Jerónimos Monastery, which is free on Sundays!

3. Viewing the sunrise and sunset.

Wherever you visit, you can find a place to view the sunrise or sunset, which happens every day and it's at no cost to you. Do some research on the best places to view this in any city.

Beautiful sunrise in Utah

4. People-watching.

One of my favorite things to do in any city is watch people. I like to find a bench, eat a snack and watch other people live their lives. If you're thinking, "that is creepy," I'd like to ask you how many shows you've watched on Netflix, which is basically watching other people live their lives. This is just doing it in person. *Tip:* wear sunglasses to avoid making direct eye-contact with people, which in my experience makes people uncomfortable.

5. Finding souvenirs.

Sure, most souvenirs cost money, however some are free! Many city visitor centers give away cool maps, post cards or other paper items you can take along. If you're at the beach, shells and other drifted items make a neat take-away. I've found cool rocks and interesting tree pieces on the ground in parks that I've kept. (I'm not sure if this is always kosher, although in Ecuador, our guide tore something off the tree and gave it to me to take home. I still have it!) If you're at a unique restaurant that you want to remember, look and see if they have sugar packets, matchbooks or napkins with their name and logo on it. I saved a sugar packet from Cafe A Brasileira because that place was awesome. And of course, my favorite souvenir: photographs. Take as many as you want... and they come with you for free!

Collecting souvenirs on the Isle of Iona in Scotland!

6. Wandering.

Never underestimate wandering. Some of my most treasured travel moments are the times when you have no plan; you just walk around and see what you find. You may see some interesting architecture, beautiful nature or see some animals. You may even meet someone new! It's fun to explore, get lost and enjoy wherever you are. And of course, it's free.

Stumbled across one of my favorite places in the world while wandering:
Chipping Campden.

7. Visiting the water-front.

Anywhere I am staying, I find myself wandering over to the water-front
areas. Not every place has this, but when they do, some of the best
people watching is there, and you get to see boats coming in and out of
the harbor. A relaxing and free thing to do!

It doesn't cost anything to watch the boats at the Lisbon water-front!

8. Meeting new people. One of the reasons I love to stay in bed and breakfasts is because you get to meet other people, talk to them and maybe even make a new friend. In Santiago, we sat around the breakfast table with people from Mexico, Paris, Germany and Brazil. Not everyone spoke English well, but somehow between all of us, we were able to use words from different languages to carry on a conversation. Pretty cool experience, and of course, it was free!

Vacation food (planning a food budget)

Food. It's one of the best parts of a vacation. However, if anything I've learned from planning a budget, it's that I almost always go over on my food budget. I guess you could say that "vacation brain" kicks in and you stop caring about how much you're spending. The other reason is that I didn't do enough menu research to figure out which restaurants I would actually dine in.

The last few vacations I've gone on, I've carefully researched and selected restaurants that I know have good reviews and where I can see a posted menu. I can use the menu to discern about how much we will spend. Surprisingly, when you're tired from sightseeing, you're OK with whatever you've picked out. I always think I don't want to plan, so I can just be spontaneous. It's fun to not plan and just figure it out, right? Sometimes. And sometimes you end up starved and arguing about where to find a restaurant at 7 p.m. and you don't know what's good or how much things cost and you finally say, "I don't care if its $400, I'm just going to eat it!" Well, if you actually plan and think about where you might be at the time of day, you can at least have some options. You can still choose to do something else, too, and be spontaneous. However, if you decide you're tired, hungry and you want to stick to a budget, you'd better pick out some places ahead of time.

Here are some suggestions for finding good restaurants around the place you'll be visiting:

1. TripAdvisor.
I'm sounding like a broken record with this TripAdvisor business. However, you can search the city you'll be in and click on the hotel/bed and breakfast you're staying at. A handy tool called "Browse nearby" opens up a map and allows you to see what's around you, including things to do. If you know you're going to a museum around lunch time, search to see if there are any restaurants that have good ratings around the museum.

2. Zagat.
These have some great reviews of restaurants in major cities (major like Paris, London, Atlanta, NYC, etc.) You can narrow down by cost, location (they have Google maps embedded) and type of food. They rate

restaurants based on decor, service and food so you can see what you're in for.

3. Google Maps.

This is a great option for finding restaurants near where you are located. If you open maps, you can click on "explore nearby" and it gives you the option for restaurants or hotels. You can see ratings, reviews and you're in a good place to see the distance it is from where you'll be.

4. Magazines and guide books.

I am old school and still read magazines for travel destinations, and they almost always review restaurants. You can find some new or funky places to try. Guidebooks are also great, especially for foreign travel. We've found some great suggestions in guidebooks when we've been in Europe and South America.

The other thing I do, besides research restaurants, is make a list of the nearest grocery stores and convenient stores. Not only is this helpful if you need to pick up some decongestants or body lotion, but also for snacks, food and water to keep in your room.

Here is an example of a grocery chart I created for a trip to the United Kingdom. I wanted places that were within walking or driving distance from the places we were staying.

GROCERY STORES

HOTEL	NAME	DISTANCE FROM HOTEL	HOURS
London	SPAR	.2 miles on Queensway	7 a.m. to 12 a.m.
	Queensway Food and Wine	.2 miles on Queensway (5 min. walk)	Mon-Sat: 24 hours Sun: 10 a.m. to 4 p.m.
Chipping Campden	One Stop	.3 miles on High St. (looks like a slight walk behind the main buildings to the left when coming from hotel)	7 a.m. to 10 p.m.
Conwy	ASDA Llandundo Junction Supermarket	1.3 miles (3 minutes in a car, over the bridge)	Mon-Sat: 7 a.m. to 10 p.m.
	Tesco Llandundo Junction	1.5 miles (4 minutes in a car, over the bridge)	Mon- Fri: 24 hours.
Keswick	Booths Supermarket	4.7 miles (13 minutes in car, in the direction of Castlerigg)	Mon-Sat: 8 a.m. to 9 p.m.
Oban	Tesco Supermarket	.4 miles (10 min walk)	Mon-Sat: 6 a.m. to midnight Sun: 8 a.m. to 10 p.m.
	Millstone Wholefoods	.4 miles (9 minute walk)	9:15 to 5:15 p.m. Closed Sun

Trip Planning Document
LOCATION NAME:
DATES:

BUDGET

WHAT	ESTIMATE COST	NOTES	ACTUAL
Plane tickets			
Additional flights			
Hotel 1			
Hotel 2			
Hotel 3			
Food, how many days		Per person/per day	
Sightseeing cost		Per person/per day	
Private tours			
Intercity transportation costs		Buses/metro, taxi	
Rental car			
Fuel for rental car			
Shopping before trip		Shoes and guidebooks	
Incidentals			
TOTAL	$		$

Total needed (estimate)	Spent	Balance

ITINERARY

Date	Time	What	Notes
Day 1			

THINGS TO DO BEFORE YOUR TRIP

What	When

SIGHTSEEING BUDGET

Where	What	Cost (per person)	Do you need to purchase ahead of time?

FOOD BUDGET

Day	Breakfast	Lunch	Dinner	Total Daily Cost

HOTEL INFORMATION

City	Hotel Name	Booked?	Cost

GROCERY STORES

Hotel	Name	Distance from Hotel

CAR RENTAL

Company Cost	Website to book Confirmation #

GUIDEBOOKS/WALKING TOUR APPS

What	Where to purchase or download

Always have a trip planned

Since I've never quit my day job to travel (I'm a part-time traveler and loving it), I'm a historian by day. One summer, we had the goal to interview many older residents in the area about their time living in our city. One woman in particular was home-bound, so we brought our video camera to her house and interviewed her in the living room. We stepped inside her kitchen, and she had those really cool peg boards on every wall with dishes, pots and kitchen utensils hanging on them (just like Julia Child). We stepped inside her living room, and it was like a world-traveler flea market's paradise. There were ponchos from South America, geisha umbrellas, miscellaneous currency, travel pictures, postcards and much more. I was mesmerized. I saw a map posted on the wall that was covered with red pins. Of course, the red pins were all the places she had been. I had trouble finding a spot on the map without a red pin. She was in her nineties. Her husband was deceased, but they spent their days working long days, and traveling on weekends. They had a station wagon they used to drive to National Parks and spend the night in the back watching the stars. As they got older, they spent more and more time on overseas adventures. They never had children, and lived in the same house for most of their life. It was a simple house, but filled with memories. She was bubbling. She was home-bound, but her travel memories surrounded her. She had other loves: church, her family, cooking. She asked me where I had been, and I told her I was just beginning to do trips here and there, but my husband and I were travel-lovers. She told me one thing I'll never forget: "Always have a trip planned." She said that knowing you have an adventure ahead of you helps you with those long days on the job and surviving these rough Ohio winters. She went on to say, "It doesn't always have to be somewhere exotic, but always have somewhere you're going next." She was in her nineties and was talking about her last trip, which was Asia, and her next trip which was Niagara Falls. I agree with her whole-heartedly. I have trips planned to many places, and I'm always ready to go. Maybe it's just a day-trip, maybe it's a two-week European excursion. But I will echo this wonderful woman and tell you the same thing: always have a trip planned. I hope this short little guide will help you to fulfill that encouragement, and you will be ready for your next adventure.

About the Author

Nina Thomas is a travel writer from Columbus, Ohio. She's been enjoying part-time travel with her husband since 2008. She's visited 15 countries, and over 125 cities. She seeks adventures ranging from camping in the wilderness to fine dining. She began writing a blog in 2014 as a way to share some of her successes, failures and travel tips that she is learning as she goes. Her goal is to share authentic experiences with others, so they can be fully empowered for their next vacation. This is her first book. She has a BA from OSU in Strategic Communication, earned her MA in Library Science and Museum Studies from Kent State University in 2017. Her passion is writing, but she also enjoys taking photographs. She lives in Westerville with her husband, Jared, and Cairn terrier, Poppy. For more practical tips from an Ohio girl, visit her website travelingwithnina.com, follow her on Instagram @travelingwithnina, follow her on Twitter @travelwithnina or check out her YouTube channel: Traveling with Nina.

TRAVELING
With Nina
Practical Travel Tips from an Ohio girl

Made in the USA
Las Vegas, NV
02 May 2024

89414901R00056